5/09

LC 8/2016

HOT

Celebrity Biographies

Hilary Duff

LIFE IN THE SPOTLIGHT

MARGIE MARKARIAN

E **Enslow Publishers, Inc.**
40 Industrial Road
Box 398
Berkeley Heights, NJ 07922
USA
http://www.enslow.com

Library of Congress Cataloging-in-Publication Data
Markarian, Margie.
  Hilary Duff : life in the spotlight / Margie Markarian.
    p. cm. — (Hot celebrity biographies)
  Includes bibliographical references and index.
  Summary: "Find out how Hilary Duff got started acting, how she became the star of a hit tv show, and what she's going to do in the future"—Provided by publisher.
  ISBN-13: 978-0-7660-3211-8
  ISBN-10: 0-7660-3211-6
  1. Duff, Hilary, 1987—Juvenile literature. 2. Actors—United States—Biography—Juvenile literature. I. Title.
  PN2287.D79M37 2009
  792.02'8'092—dc22
  [B]
                          2008026464

Paperback ISBN-13: 978-0-7660-3211-8
Paperback ISBN-10: 0-7660-3626-0

Printed in the United States of America

10 9 8 7 6 5 4 3 2 1

To our readers: We have done our best to make sure all Internet Addresses in this book were active and appropriate when we went to press. However, the author and the publisher have no control over and assume no liability for the material available on those Internet sites or on other Web sites they may link to. Any comments or suggestions can be sent by e-mail to comments@enslow.com or to the address on the back cover.

♻ Enslow Publishers, Inc., is committed to printing our books on recycled paper. The paper in every book contains 10% to 30% post-consumer waste (PCW). The cover board on the outside of each book contains 100% PCW. Our goal is to do our part to help young people and the environment too!

Photographs: Jason DeCrow/AP Images 1, 26; Tammie Arroyo/AP Images, 4; Chris Pizzello/AP Images, 7, 8, 23, 32; Richard Drew/AP Images, 9; Luis Martinez/AP Images, 11; Krista Niles/AP Images, 12, 13; Jim Spellman/WireImage/Getty Images, 15; Robert Mora/Getty Images, 17; Frank Gunn/AP Images, 19; Michelle Cop/Getty Images, 20; Rob Griffith/AP Images, 21; Nam Y. Huh/AP Images, 25; Jason DeCrow/AP Images, 26; PRNewsWire/AP Images, 28; Jeff Christensen/AP Images, 31; Mark J. Terrill/AP Images, 34; Susan Walsh/AP Images, 37, 40; Matt Sayles/AP Images, 43

Cover photo: Hilary Duff appears onstage during MTV's *Total Request Live* in 2007. Jason DeCrow/AP Images.

Contents

An Entertaining Start

How does it feel to go to bed one night and wake up a celebrity the next day? Hilary Duff knows. She became famous overnight at age thirteen. That was the night the first episode of *Lizzie McGuire* aired on the Disney Channel in January 2001.

The show was an instant hit. Audiences fell in love with the character of Lizzie, an ordinary middle school girl with a sunny personality. They also fell in love with Hilary, the bubbly teenager who played Lizzie. Soon she was starring in movies, recording CDs, and posing for magazine covers.

The top-rated show ended in 2004 after sixty-five episodes. But Hilary stays in the spotlight with more movies and sold-out concerts. In between gigs, Hilary designs clothes for her stylish 'tween fashion line and writes songs for her next CD. Her exciting career just keeps moving in new directions.

Hilary got started in show business early. She was born on September 28, 1987, to Bob and Susan Duff. A big sister,

◀ *Hilary Duff, pictured here at Nickelodeon's Seventeenth Annual Kids' Choice Awards in 2004, has gone on to win several awards.*

IT'S A SISTER THING

Some sisters are competitive and jealous of each other's successes. Not Hilary and Haylie Duff. These two sisters are the best of friends.

Hilary has always looked up to Haylie. "She is so beautiful on the inside and outside," said Hilary. Her big sister is always right there "if I need somebody to talk to, or if I need advice, if I'm having a problem, if I want to goof off and laugh and smile."

The two had a great time together starring in *Material Girls* and singing "Our Lips Are Sealed" for the soundtrack to *A Cinderella Story*. Haylie also writes songs for Hilary's albums.

Although Haylie's acting career hasn't brought her the same kind of fame as Hilary, she has had many successes. Maybe you've seen her in reruns of *Seventh Heaven*. She played Sandy Jameson from 2005 to 2007. She was also in the movie *Napoleon Dynamite* and recently spent several months in the cast of *Hairspray* on Broadway as Amber Von Tussle, a mean girl. She had a recurring role as Amy on the *Lizzie McGuire* show, too.

Haylie, was waiting for her at home in Houston, Texas. The Duff girls were only two years apart and became best friends. Almost from the time Hilary started walking, they provided the household entertainment. The sisters would sing, dance, and act out their favorite TV shows around the house.

Hilary looked up to her older sister and wanted to be just like her. When Haylie started taking dancing lessons, Hilary decided, "Me too!" She must have been a pretty good little dancer. A touring ballet company came to town looking for young ballerinas to dance in the show *The Nutcracker*. The ballet

▲ *Hilary Duff first got into acting because she wanted to be like her big sister Haylie* (left).

company picked six-year-old Hilary and eight-year-old Haylie to be in the show!

Acting classes came next. First it was Haylie, then Hilary. Haylie had so much fun, Hilary wanted to do it too. She wanted to be just like her older sister.

The girls were so enthusiastic about acting and dancing that the Duffs moved to San Antonio, Texas. There, the girls attended a private school that offered daily classes in acting, music, and dance. Hilary's first job was in a TV ad.

▲ *Since* Lizzie McGuire *ended, Hilary Duff has continued acting and singing.*

CALIFORNIA DREAMING

Sometimes Hollywood directors came to Texas to make movies. The Duff sisters tried out for whatever roles were available for girls their age. Both of them had small parts in *True Women*, a television mini-series that starred Angelina Jolie.

Young Hilary and Haylie quickly realized there were not many acting opportunities in Texas. They started asking their parents if they could go to Hollywood, California. Their parents weren't so sure. No one in the family had ever been in show business. Bob ran a chain of small stores. Susan was a stay-at-home mom. Living in Hollywood would be a lot different from living on a Texas ranch.

Finally, Bob and Susan agreed to let their daughters try their luck in Hollywood. "Our parents have always been super-supportive of whatever we wanted to do, which is cool," Hilary told *Interview* magazine.

At first, Susan and the girls went to California for short periods of time during pilot season. Pilot season is when TV shows cast actors and actresses for new shows they plan to create. Bob stayed in Texas but visited every three weeks.

The very first time Susan took the girls to California, she was tricked. She paid a large sum of money to a woman who said she could arrange auditions. The woman lied, and the Duffs lost their money.

Susan then learned all she could about breaking into show business—finding an agent, going on auditions, and signing contracts. Things went much better, but it still wasn't easy to get noticed. In Hollywood, there was a lot of competition for the small number of

▶ *While she got her start in acting, Hilary Duff's other true passion is music.*

jobs for girls their age. Hilary went on many auditions but mostly got more TV ads. That is still a huge accomplishment, of course, and a chance many people never get!

SOME OPPORTUNITIES, SOME SETBACKS

In 1997, Hilary landed her first big job. She won a starring role in the live-action movie *Casper Meets Wendy*. She played Wendy, a good witch. Her cartoon co-star was Casper the Friendly Ghost. Together, Casper and Wendy prevent an evil wizard from destroying Wendy and her three wacky witch aunts. The role earned Hilary a nomination for a Young Actress Award.

Hilary's next role was in the 1999 TV movie *Soul Collector*. Now twelve, Hilary was nominated for an award again. This time, she took home a trophy for Best Supporting Young Actress. The Duffs thought success was just around the corner. But it wasn't. Despite the recognition and many more auditions, Hilary did not receive any important acting offers for about two years.

The Duffs started thinking about packing up and going back to Texas. Then, a promising opportunity came Hilary's way. Hilary was chosen to play one of the kids in a show called *Daddio*. The show's producers had high hopes for *Daddio* because it starred Michael Chiklis, a well-known actor.

▲ *Actress Hilary Duff almost gave up her dream of acting before snagging the "Lizzie McGuire" role.*

The NBC network picked the show for its spring 2000 lineup. There was a sad casting change, though. The producers didn't want Hilary! They decided she wasn't right for the part.

Becoming "Lizzie McGuire"

Not being chosen for *Daddio* was a huge disappointment for twelve-year-old Duff. She was very close to giving up her dream of becoming an actress. Duff wasn't even sure she wanted to try out for a new Disney show called *What's Lizzie Thinking?* She had no idea she was on the verge of stardom.

The creators of *What's Lizzie Thinking?* had an unusual format in mind for the show. They needed an actress who could play an ordinary middle school girl with a cartoon sidekick. The character was not especially popular, athletic, or smart. But she was likable, pretty, and stylish. They also wanted the actress to be lively enough to be the voice of the cartoonish sidekick. The cartoon version of Lizzie would pop up during the show. She would say the things the real Lizzie was too polite or embarrassed to say out loud.

During an interview with *Seventeen* magazine, Duff and her sister recalled the audition process. "There were two hundred blonde girls exactly like me auditioning for Lizzie," she said. "I kept wearing all these crazy outfits to the auditions. I identified with Lizzie. Lizzie McGuire was me—I was awkward, kind of clumsy."

"But hip and happening," added her sister, Haylie.

It took Duff four auditions to clinch the job. The show's producer, Stan Rogow, explained how Disney chose Duff.

▲ *Hilary Duff, pictured on set, won Disney over with her fun personality.* ▶

13

During an interview with the *Los Angeles Daily News*, he said, "Each time we saw Duff, she was more interesting to watch. So, while the auditioning process can be painful, part of what's revealed is who you're not getting bored with. Slowly, you began not to be able to take your eyes off Duff. It became, 'That's the girl.'"

ON THE SET

The name of the show was changed to *Lizzie McGuire*. Filming started in the summer of 2000. When the show debuted in January 2001, it quickly became a big hit. An average of two million people tuned in on Friday nights. They wanted to find out what Lizzie's latest problem would be and how she and her best friends would solve it.

Viewers, especially girls between the ages of eight and fourteen, adored Lizzie. She was a normal teen trying to figure out who she was and where she fit in. They related to her worries about what to wear on picture day, being paired with a geek in health class, and becoming tongue-tied around cute boys.

"She's the kind of girl nobody notices at first," is how Duff described Lizzie to the *Los Angeles Daily News*. "She doesn't know how charismatic she really is."

MEET THE CAST OF LIZZIE McGUIRE!

While filming, Hilary Duff spent long days on the set with her circle of *Lizzie McGuire* friends and family. Here's who they were:

David "Gordo" Gordon: Lizzie's brainy filmmaker friend was played by the curly-haired Adam Lamberg. In *The Lizzie McGuire Movie*, Gordo and Lizzie finally realize they have a romantic interest in each other!

Miranda Sanchez: This devoted BFF had a talent for playing the violin and getting Lizzie out of sticky situations. Miranda was played by Lalaine Vergara-Paras.

Matt McGuire: Matt was known for his crafty pranks. Actor Jake Thomas was an expert at annoying big sister Lizzie when the cameras were rolling!

Mom "Jo" McGuire: Hallie Todd played Lizzie's mom. Her good intentions did not always work out as expected, but she and Lizzie were close.

Dad "Sam" McGuire: Lizzie's Dad, who was played by the actor Robert Carradine, was mostly clueless about raising a teenage daughter, but his love never faltered.

▲ *Hilary Duff autographs a poster for* The Lizzie McGuire Movie.

Duff enjoyed being on a hit TV show, but it was hard work. She was on the set more than nine hours each day.

"I get up at 5:30 a.m., so I'm on the set by 7:00 a.m. Then it's wardrobe, hair, and makeup until 8:30, and I either begin three hours of schoolwork with my teacher or shoot our first scene," Duff told *Girls' Life* magazine. "Thirty minutes for lunch, then animated Lizzie lines, back to shooting, and we end around 4:30. I have homework, lines to learn, and Tae-Bo [exercise routine]. I get to bed by 9:30!"

During the time she worked on *Lizzie McGuire*, Duff probably spent more hours with her cast mates on the set than with her own family at home.

DEALING WITH FAME

Being on a popular TV show was a dream come true for Duff. But it did affect her personal life. Suddenly, people recognized her wherever she went. Going out with her friends to the movies, restaurants, or the mall became more difficult. Fans would come up to her to ask her to sign something or take pictures. The attention has made it harder to just kick back, but she has gotten used to it and always tries to be friendly to her fans.

▲ *Hilary Duff and Lalaine Vergara-Paras (left)* help at a Boys and Girls Club.

"They're the people who let me do what I love to do every day, so it's much easier to be nice to them than it is to be rude," she told *YM* magazine when she was sixteen years old. "Sometimes I'll say, 'Oh, I'm just hanging out with my friends being normal right now, so thanks for watching the show.'"

Part of being an actress involves doing publicity. So, even when Duff wasn't working on the set, she was often working somewhere. She appeared on talk shows and hosted award shows. She also interviewed with magazines, chatted online with fans, and attended special events.

BRANCHING OUT

The success of *Lizzie McGuire* let Duff explore other parts of show business. Disney cast her in the made-for-TV movie *Cadet Kelly*. In this 2002 film, Duff played a creative, free-spirited girl. The character has to move to a new town and attend a strict military school when her mom marries a military officer. Since Duff is very athletic, she had fun going to "boot camp" to learn how cadets train.

Cadet Kelly was a ratings smash and led to more movie roles. Duff's first big-screen movie was *Agent Cody Banks,* starring Frankie Muniz from the TV show *Malcolm in the Middle.* In this movie, Duff played Natalie, the girl Cody secretly likes. Another movie appearance for Duff was *Cheaper by the Dozen*, with Steve Martin as the father of a family with twelve kids. Duff was one of the dozen children.

Of course, the biggest thrill was starring in *The Lizzie McGuire Movie.* Duff played two parts—Lizzie and a Lizzie-look-alike Italian singer named Isabella. The excitement included a trip to Italy to shoot the movie. Duff got to ride around Rome on a motor scooter with her handsome co-star and sing several songs for the soundtrack album. The album ended up selling more than one million copies! That was good news for Duff's budding singing career.

Moving in New Directions

The songs Duff sang for the soundtrack of *The Lizzie McGuire Movie* in 2003 were not her very first recordings. Duff started thinking about a singing career after being backstage at a Radio Disney concert in 2001. She was impressed and inspired by what she saw and heard.

She started working with a voice coach.

About a year later, Duff took some small steps toward the start of her musical career. She recorded the song "Tiki, Tiki, Tiki Room" for the first *DisneyMania* CD and a Christmas album called *Santa Claus Lane*. The title song of the holiday album was even featured in Disney's *The Santa Clause 2* movie. Duff also recorded "I Can't Wait" for the *Lizzie McGuire* TV show soundtrack. The single quickly became a number one hit on Radio Disney.

These positive experiences set the stage for Duff's first pop album, *Metamorphosis*. The word metamorphosis means change. That's exactly what happened to Duff's career when the album was released in the summer of 2003. The album made Duff into a pop music star. The album and the song "So Yesterday" went straight to the top of the charts. To date, more than 3.7 million copies of the album have been sold.

Soon Duff was performing in live concerts, shooting music videos, and making appearances on MTV's *TRL* (Total Request Live). The interaction with the audience was both thrilling and rewarding. "It's so cool to be onstage and have people sing your songs back to you," she told *Interview* magazine. "There's no feeling like that."

She explained the difference between singing and acting to *Girl's Life* magazine in this way: "I'm excited about my album because it's not characters I'm playing, it's me. It's more personal than acting. . . . All the songs have so much to do with my personal life."

GOOD-BYE, *LIZZIE MCGUIRE*

Music and movie-making soon became the focus of Duff's career. That's because her days as "Lizzie McGuire" came to a close. Even though the show and movie were very popular, Disney and the Duffs could not agree on a new contract. Fans were sad that the series wouldn't follow Lizzie through high school, but it wasn't the last they would see of Duff!

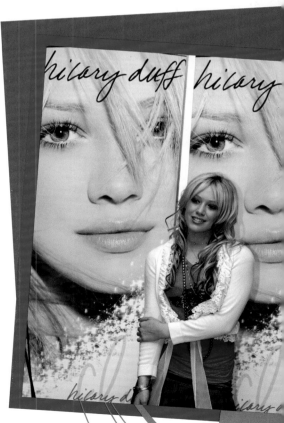

▲ *Hilary Duff promotes her album* Hilary Duff *and the movie* Raise Your Voice *in 2004.* ▶

HILARY'S MUSIC CAREER

Children's Music
DisneyMania (2002)
Santa Claus Lane (2002)
DisneyMania 2 (2004)

TV/Movie Soundtracks
The Lizzie McGuire Soundtrack (2002)
The Lizzie McGuire Movie Soundtrack (2003)
A Cinderella Story Soundtrack (2004)

Pop Albums
Metamorphosis (2003)
Hilary Duff (2004)
Hilary Duff Most Wanted (2005)
Dignity (2007)

Duff already was working on new movie deals. In 2004, she starred in *A Cinderella Story* and *Raise Your Voice*. *A Cinderella Story* was a modern remake of Duff's favorite fairy tale. Even though critics didn't like the movie, it earned more than $50 million at the box office. Duff even won a Teen Choice Award for Choice Movie Blush Scene.

Duff's fans enjoyed seeing her as Samantha in *A Cinderella Story*. The character is a serious student and hard-working waitress who wants to go to Princeton University. They also enjoyed seeing her win the love of a Prince Charming who chats online and uses a lost cell phone to track her down. Duff sang five of the fourteen songs on the movie's soundtrack, including "Our Lips Are Sealed" with her sister Haylie.

The movie *Raise Your Voice* wasn't as successful at the box office, but it was still a great experience for Duff. She filmed it in early 2004 when *Metamorphosis* was really hot. She had to learn how to balance the responsibilities of two demanding careers.

"You just do it. It's like I want to be able to do all of these things, and I have to be really prepared to do it. It doesn't really bother me, every day thinking that I'm going to have to switch modes to singing or acting or traveling, or this, that, and the other. You just kind of do it. It's just kind of natural."

▼ *While she enjoys acting, Hilary Duff loves the thrill of performing for a live audience during her concerts.*

MORE MOVIES AND MORE MUSIC

With that kind of attitude, Duff's career moved full speed ahead. Her next movies were *The Perfect Man*, *Cheaper by the Dozen 2*, and *Material Girls*. In *The Perfect Man*, Duff played a sweet but scheming daughter who matches up her lovelorn mother with the ideal mate. Of course, there are funny accidents and mix-ups along the way!

The laughs continued in the sequel to *Cheaper by the Dozen*. Duff repeated her role as Lorraine, one of twelve kids in the crazy Baker clan. But Duff probably had the most fun making *Material Girls*. That's because Duff got to star in it with Haylie. The two of them played rich, spoiled sisters who suddenly find themselves poor and homeless. They spend the rest of the movie trying to win back control of the makeup company their father left them. Along the way, they become much nicer people.

In between working on movies, Duff released two more albums. She also went on concert tours in the United States, Canada, Europe, Australia, and Japan. An album titled *Hilary Duff* came out on her seventeenth birthday. It had more of a rock sound than *Metamorphosis* and didn't sell as well.

About a year later, things bounced back with the release of a greatest hits album called *Most Wanted*. It featured three new songs, including the big hit "Wake Up." Her collaborators on

HILARY ONSCREEN

TV Movies
Casper Meets Wendy (1998)
Soul Collector (1999)
Cadet Kelly (2002)

Big-Screen Movies
Cheaper by the Dozen
    (2003)
Agent Cody Banks (2003)
The Lizzie McGuire Movie
    (2003)
A Cinderella Story (2004)
Raise Your Voice (2004)
The Perfect Man (2005)
Cheaper by the Dozen 2
    (2005)
Material Girls (2006)

▲ *Hilary Duff arrives at the 31st annual American Music Awards in 2003.*

this project included her sister and her boyfriend at the time, Joel Madden, and his twin brother Benji. Joel and Benji are from the punk-rock band Good Charlotte.

An Ambitious Teen

Duff's success in the entertainment world created many new opportunities for her in the business world. Some of the most exciting ones involved toys, games, and fashion.

The makers of *The Sims*™ video games found out that Duff was a big fan of their games. They invited her to help them create a Hilary Duff character for one of their games. Her pet Chihuahua, Lola, got to be a character too!

"I've logged hundreds of hours playing *The Sims* games, so I jumped at the chance to be in *The Sims 2 Pets*," Duff mentioned on the game's Web site. "I love creating Sims characters and guiding them through life."

That same year, she helped the Mattel toy company create two Hilary Duff Barbie® dolls. One doll wore a fancy dress. She looked ready to attend a Hollywood awards event. The other doll was dressed casually in denim for a day of shopping with her sister doll. If you're thinking the sister doll was modeled after Haylie, you guessed right. The Duff dolls

◄ *In addition to her singing and acting abilities, Duff has become known for her fashion sense. She even has her own fashion line.*

came out around the same time *Material Girls* hit movie theaters in 2006.

Besides lending her famous face to the dolls line, Duff also starred in Barbie® TV ads, created Barbie outfits, and hosted a Barbie fashion show. Mattel executive Jamie Wood explained why he paired Duff with the character of Barbie. He said the two of them are "great role models to girls and the perfect design duo. . . . They also show girls there are no limits to what they can do."

FASHION AND FRAGRANCE

Duff's reputation for style and fashion goes way beyond creating outfits for dolls. Her famous face has been on the cover of many fashion magazines, such as *Seventeen, Teen, Teen Vogue, CosmoGIRL!, Cosmopolitan, Self,* and *Vanity Fair.* She even got to be a guest editor at *Seventeen.*

Duff also has created a fashion line for 'tweens. *Women's Wear Daily*, a well-respected news journal on women's fashion, described the clothes as "girly, youthful, and fun." Parents will be happy, too. Girls will be able to look good, while still being covered. "Looking good and being trendy shouldn't mean showing off a lot of skin," Duff told the *Canadian Press* when she introduced the line at a fashion show in Toronto in 2004. "The clothes can let girls be creative and have fun fashions without being super revealing."

With help from the beauty products company Elizabeth Arden, Duff also has created her own perfumes. Her first perfume was so popular that a second scent came out about a year later.

DOWNSIDE OF FAME

Although being a celebrity has many benefits, it also has some drawbacks. Duff knows them all too well. For a while, Duff was troubled by articles about her weight being too high or too low. "There definitely was a time when I was pretty obsessed with my weight, but I'm better off not stressing about my body all the time," she told *Cosmopolitan* magazine. "It's not attractive when girls get super-skinny. . . . You lose some happiness when that's all you think about." She maintains a healthy weight by eating a balanced diet and exercising regularly.

AWESOME SWEET 16 BIRTHDAY BASH

Talk about a great birthday! When Duff turned Sweet Sixteen, she thought she was going to Hawaii to relax with her family and perform in her first live concert. When she arrived, she was shocked and delighted to learn that her six best friends had been flown in too. The adventure-filled vacation ended up being filmed for a TV special called *Hilary Duff's Island Birthday Bash*.

Besides swimming, boating, and surfing, the fun included exploring caves, driving all-terrain vehicles, rope swinging, kayaking, and scuba diving. Duff and her friends also jumped off rocks into beautiful lagoons. And of course, they did lots of laughing and singing by the campfire.

The highlight of the trip was Duff's concert performance. She sang songs from *Metamorphosis*, which had just been released. When the birthday cake arrived, everyone sang birthday wishes to Hilary. A food fight even broke out onstage! "It was definitely my best birthday ever," Duff said.

In Style magazine once asked her how she deals with the pressure of looking fashionable all the time. "I try not to be obsessed with it," she said. "People are never completely satisfied with you. One person will like what you are wearing, and another person won't. . . . It can be hard, but I try to forget what they say."

The more well known Duff became, the more she had to cope with a lack of privacy. She also has faced rumors and mean-spirited stories in the news. She tries hard not to let it bother her too much. It isn't always easy, though.

One situation that Duff could not just shake off was a man stalking her. She had to go to court to stop an eighteen-year-old man from following her and making threats. He was eventually sentenced to 117 days in jail and five years probation. Charges against a second stalker, a fifty-year-old photographer, were dropped after he apologized. He promised not to contact Duff again and helped police build a case against the man who went to jail.

A lack of privacy from the paparazzi also made it more difficult for Duff to deal with her parents' divorce in 2007 and her break-up with former boyfriend Joel Madden in 2006. When she started dating National Hockey League player Mike Comrie in 2007, photographers tried snapping pictures of the couple out in public.

▼ *Hilary Duff signs an autograph after a performance in 2005. Duff always tries to be friendly to her fans.*

▲ *Sisters Haylie* (left) *and Hilary Duff have stayed close friends despite their different career paths.*

ACTING WITH DIGNITY

Through all the ups and downs of being a celebrity, Duff tries to be gracious and friendly. Unlike many of her peers in Hollywood, she is not much of a party girl. She has a strong support system that includes her family, management team, and longtime friends. She's very close to her mother and sister. In fact, she shares a house with Haylie, and her mom lives only five houses away.

Throughout her teen years, Duff was always very aware of being a good role model for young girls. Since Duff has become an adult, her music has taken on a more mature sound. She has started pursuing more mature acting roles. However, she still intends to be a good role model and lead her life with self-respect. In fact, her latest album is titled *Dignity*. During an interview with *Billboard* magazine, she explained that it is a quality she strives to possess. "It's also something that can be easily lost. I hope I can hold on to dignity as I move forward."

Giving Back and Looking Forward

Duff makes a point of giving back to others. Volunteer and charity work are very important to her. She has been especially devoted to USA Harvest, Kids with a Cause, and Return to Freedom. She credits her mom for giving her a passion to help others.

As Duff said during an interview with PBS *Kids Go!* a few years ago: "My mom is into charity. If we have a dinner party or a birthday party, she tells people, 'Don't bring presents for us. Bring diapers or something so we can give it away.'"

Through USA Harvest, Duff helps collect and distribute food to people in need. She encourages restaurants, hospitals, and food suppliers to donate their extra food to help the poor. She also asks fans to bring boxed and canned food items to her concerts.

USA Harvest guesses that Duff has helped collect more than four million pounds of food! Duff gives hands-on help too.

◀ *Hilary Duff accepts her award for Favorite Movie Actress at Nickelodeon's Eighteenth Annual Kids' Choice Awards in 2005.*

On the first anniversary of Hurricane Katrina, Duff served hundreds of meals at a shelter in New Orleans.

Duff is also committed to Kids with a Cause. This group reaches out to kids all over the world who are in need. They may be poor, hungry, sick, abused, or uneducated. She helps by visiting sick children in hospitals, going to theme parks with disadvantaged youths, and raising money and awareness.

Duff grew up on a ranch and loves animals. So it's not surprising that she wanted to get involved with Return to Freedom, a sanctuary for wild horses. She was inspired to help after meeting Spirit, the horse who was the model for the animated horse in the movie *Spirit: Stallion of the Cimarron*. She was the official Youth Ambassador for Return to Freedom from 2003 to 2005.

Duff also cares deeply about military families. Through the Armed Forces Foundation, she visits military hospitals and invites military families to attend her concerts.

She summed up her feelings about helping others on the Return to Freedom Web site. "I think it's really important to give back to your community—and it makes you feel so good to get involved with a charity. I look up to people who are involved with organizations that help people and animals."

WINNING AWARDS AND RECOGNITION

Since she was young, Duff has been winning awards. Her first was a Young Artist Award in 2000 for work in a TV movie. At the height of her *Lizzie McGuire* fame, Duff was nominated for Nickelodeon's Kids Choice Awards year after year. She actually won four years in a row! In 2002 and 2003, *Lizzie McGuire* was named Favorite TV Show. In 2004, Duff won Favorite Female Singer. That was followed

▼ *Hilary Duff prepares to read a book to a group of children during an event for National Military Family Week.*

DUFF'S FAVORITE CHARITIES

Armed Forces Foundation
Provides financial support for service members and their families.

Kids with a Cause
Connects young celebrities with children in need.

Return to Freedom
Protects the freedom and natural lifestyle of wild horses.

USA Harvest
Collects surplus food from restaurants, hospitals, and food suppliers.

by Favorite Movie Actress in 2005 for *The Lizzie McGuire Movie*.

The singer and actress has become a familiar face at the Teen Choice Awards on Fox. She hosted the show twice and won awards three times. The first time, she won Breakout Star for *The Lizzie McGuire Movie* (2003). The next time she won Choice Movie Blush Scene for *A Cinderella Story* (2005). Most recently, she took home a Teen Choice Award in the Love Song category for "With Love" (2007).

Duff also has been noticed for her moneymaking abilities. *Forbes*, a top business magazine, has considered Duff one of the world's best-paid young celebrities for the past several years. In 2007, the magazine estimated that she was earning

$12 million for a year's work. The magazine placed her seventh in its list of the "Twenty Top-Earning Young Superstars." In 2008, *Forbes* named her one of the "Twenty Cash Queens of Music."

STILL GOING STRONG

Duff has big plans for the future. She wants to do more singing, songwriting, acting, and fashion designing. She's especially proud of the work she did on *Dignity* because she co-wrote all fourteen songs. The album has received a lot of praise from experts in the music industry.

As Sharon Dastur, the program director for one of New York's top radio stations, told *Billboard* magazine: "My first reaction watching the video for 'With Love' was 'This is exactly the kind of song she should be doing.' Duff's more mature look completed the package. Her sound and image are a natural progression."

Duff also filmed three more movies in 2007 and 2008. The first one was an animated movie called *Foodfight!* The story was set in a supermarket that comes to life at night. Duff voiced the role of Sunshine Goodness, while her sister, Haylie, voiced the role of Sweet Cakes.

▲ *Hilary Duff greets a cancer patient during an event in Washington, D.C. Duff makes a point of giving back to others.*

On a more serious note, Duff starred in *War, Inc.* with John Cusack, who wrote the script. At first Duff wasn't interested in the job because she didn't want to play a teen pop star. But after reading the script, she realized that the role was very different from anything she had done before. The character of Yonica is a dark-haired Russian pop singer who lives a very dangerous life. Plus, John Cusack actually created the character with Duff in mind. How flattering!

AND THE WINNER IS...

The Emmys and Oscars aren't the only awards actors can hope to win. Several award shows have been created specifically to honor the work of young people. In 1978, the Young Artist Foundation started giving out Young Artist Awards to performers under age eighteen. Later came the Nickelodeon Kids' Choice Awards, which started in 1986. As you might have guessed from the name, kids vote on the winners. Similarly, the Teen Choice Awards are voted on by teens. The first Teen Choice Awards aired in 1999. That's the same year the Young Hollywood Awards started recognizing young stars.

Hilary Duff has been recognized by all four, either as a nominee or a winner. She has been nominated more than a dozen times. Here are the awards she has won.

2005
- Kids' Choice Award for Favorite Movie Actress for *A Cinderella Story*
- Teen Choice Award for Choice Movie Blush Scene for *A Cinderella Story*

2004
- Young Artist Award for Best Young Ensemble in a Feature Film for *Cheaper by the Dozen* (shared with other young cast members)
- Young Hollywood Award for Today's Superstar

2003
- Teen Choice Award for Choice Movie Breakout Star for *The Lizzie McGuire Movie*

2000
- Young Artist Award for Best Performance in a TV Movie or Pilot by a Supporting Young Actress for *The Soul Collector*

She also filmed *Greta* in 2007. It is a coming-of-age story about an unhappy teenager who is sent to live with her grandparents for the summer. Duff enjoyed acting in this challenging role. It was so different from the types of roles she's been known for, and the type of person that she is.

Hilary Duff has a bright future ahead of her. The young girl who used to be "Lizzie McGuire" has entered her twenties and already has had many successes. She has starred in a hit TV show, sold more than 13 million records, and filmed fourteen movies. Not to mention, she's overseen several successful business projects and done important charity work. Duff works hard and is proud of her accomplishments. And, she appreciates the people who have helped her come so far in such a short time. She's definitely one lucky girl, and she knows it!

Hilary Duff plans to stay busy. Fans can expect to see ▶ more music and movies in the years to come.

Timeline

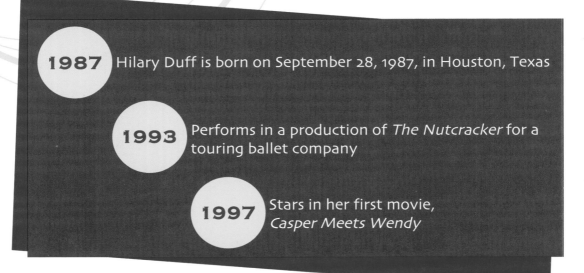

1987 — Hilary Duff is born on September 28, 1987, in Houston, Texas

1993 — Performs in a production of *The Nutcracker* for a touring ballet company

1997 — Stars in her first movie, *Casper Meets Wendy*

2000 — Wins Young Artist Award for supporting actress work in *Soul Collector*, a TV movie

2001 — First episode of *Lizzie McGuire* airs on Disney Channel

2002 — Releases her first album, *Santa Claus Lane*

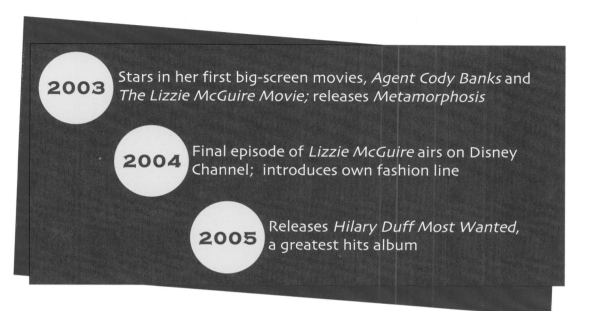

2003 Stars in her first big-screen movies, *Agent Cody Banks* and *The Lizzie McGuire Movie;* releases *Metamorphosis*

2004 Final episode of *Lizzie McGuire* airs on Disney Channel; introduces own fashion line

2005 Releases *Hilary Duff Most Wanted*, a greatest hits album

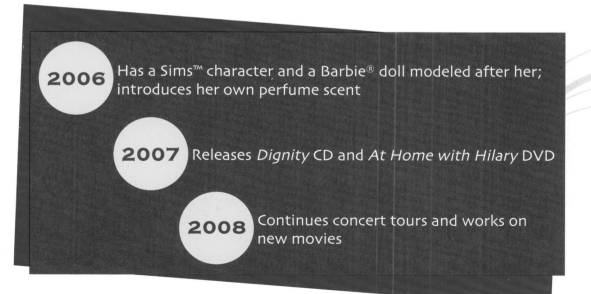

2006 Has a Sims™ character and a Barbie® doll modeled after her; introduces her own perfume scent

2007 Releases *Dignity* CD and *At Home with Hilary* DVD

2008 Continues concert tours and works on new movies

Further Info

Books

Israel, Elaine. *Hilary Duff*. Strongsville, OH: Gareth Stevens Publishing, 2007.

Rettenmund, Matthew. *Hilary Duff: All Access*. New York: The Berkley Publishing Group, 2005.

Whiting, Jim. *Hilary Duff: A View from the Paparazzi*. Broomall, PA: Mason Crest Publishers, Inc., 2008.

CDs and DVDs

Hilary Duff Dignity Deluxe Edition (Audio CD and DVD featuring At Home with Hilary Duff Interview). Hollywood Records, 2007.

Metamorphosis (Audio CD). Buena Vista, 2003.

The Lizzie McGuire Show Boxed DVD Set—Volume One (2001). Dir. David Carradine, et. al. Walt Disney Home Entertainment, 2004.

Internet Addresses

Hilary Duff's official Web site
http://www.hilaryduff.com

The Internet Movie Database: Hilary Duff
http://www.imdb.com/name/nm0240381/

Glossary

audition—Short performance that tests an entertainer's abilities.

charismatic—Fascinating, charming, or appealing.

collaborators—People who work together to do something.

contracts—Legal agreements made in writing.

debuted—Appeared for the first time.

dignity—Self-respect, honor.

metamorphosis—A change or transformation.

nomination—Being selected for the chance to win a prize, award, or election.

paparazzi—A photographer who takes pictures of celebrities.

sanctuary—A safe place.

stalking—Following or contacting someone repeatedly in a threatening way. This behavior is usually unwanted and can be illegal.

Index